Shaun the Sheep™

Too Many Jobs!

Series Director: Richard (Golly) Goleszowski
Adapted by Monica Hughes

The farmer was sick, so he went to bed.

Shaun had to do all the jobs on the farm.

There was too much to do!

The sheep had to help Shaun.

The sheep went to get the eggs ...

but a goat bumped the sheep.
All the eggs fell out of the box!

Oh no!

So Shaun had to get the eggs.

The sheep went to get the milk ...

but the sheep got stuck!

Oh no!

So Shaun had to get the milk.

The sheep had to drive the tractor ...

but the tractor fell into the pool!

Oh no!

When the farmer was well,
he got out of bed.

He went to look at the farm.
"Thank you, Shaun," he said ...

but he did not see the tractor!

Oops!